LE CORDON BLEU

HOME COLLECTION

·FINGER FOOD·

MEREHURST

contents

recipe ratings ⚜ *easy*   ⚜⚜ *a little more care needed*   ⚜⚜⚜ *more care needed*

Salmon, prawn and avocado rolls

These rolls are extremely simple to prepare and require no cooking. To ensure excellent results, the ingredients must be of the finest quality.

Preparation time **25 minutes**
Total cooking time **Nil**
Makes 32

300 g (10 oz) smoked salmon slices
1/2 avocado
1 tablespoon lemon juice
16 medium cooked prawns, peeled and deveined
lumpfish roe, to garnish
fresh dill, to garnish

1 Cut the salmon slices into 3 x 5 cm (1¹/4 x 2 inch) rectangles. Remove the stone from the avocado half, cut in two and remove the skin. Then cut each quarter into four or five slices lengthways and cut the slices in half through the middle. Place the pieces in a bowl and toss in the lemon juice.
2 Roll a piece of avocado or a prawn in each piece of salmon and place on a serving tray. Decorate the rolls with some lumpfish roe and a sprig of dill.

Chef's tip These rolls can be prepared several hours in advance. Once assembled, cover with plastic wrap and store in the refrigerator.

Cheese stuffed mushrooms

These firm raw mushrooms with a soft mixed herb and garlic cream cheese filling are easy to prepare and delicious to eat. If making large quantities, it is quicker to use a piping bag to fill the mushrooms.

Preparation time **20 minutes**
Total cooking time **5 minutes**
Makes about **20**

200 g (6¹/2 oz) even-sized button mushrooms
I small clove garlic, halved
120 g (4 oz) cream cheese
2 tablespoons chopped mixed fresh herbs, such as parsley, chives and thyme
I teaspoon lemon juice
fresh chervil or parsley leaves or chopped fresh garlic chives, to garnish

1 Remove any dirt from the mushrooms with your fingers and lightly wipe with a clean soft cloth to remove any remaining dirt. Cut the stems from the mushrooms and discard.

2 Put the garlic halves into a small saucepan and cover with water. Bring to the boil, simmer for 3 minutes, then drain. Crush the garlic and put into a small bowl. Add the cream cheese, mixed herbs and lemon juice and mix together until smooth. Season generously with salt and freshly ground black pepper.

3 Spoon the filling into a piping bag fitted with a small star nozzle and pipe into each mushroom. Alternatively, use a teaspoon to fill each mushroom with the cheese and herb mixture until it comes slightly over the top of the mushroom.

4 Arrange the stuffed mushrooms on a serving dish, cover loosely with plastic wrap and chill until ready to serve. Each mushroom can be decorated with either a small leaf of chervil or parsley or a sprinkling of chopped garlic chives. Alternatively, you could decorate the mushrooms with a small diamond-shaped piece of tomato to add colour.

Chicken liver pâté

A simply made pâté dip with lots of flavour. If you want a stronger flavour, try making it with duck liver.

*Preparation time **15 minutes + 15 minutes cooling***
*Total cooking time **10 minutes***
*Serves **4 as an appetiser***

115 g (3³/₄ oz) unsalted butter, at room temperature
2 French shallots, finely chopped
2 cloves garlic, finely chopped
225 g (7¹/₄ oz) chicken liver, trimmed
sprig of fresh thyme
bay leaf
large pinch each of ground nutmeg, clove and
   cinnamon
1 tablespoon brandy or port
2 tablespoons cream or crème fraîche

1 Place 30 g (1 oz) of the butter in a frying pan and add the shallots and garlic. Cook over a gentle heat until they soften and turn transparent.
2 Over medium heat, add the liver, thyme, bay leaf, spices and some salt and pepper to the shallot mixture. Fry for 3 minutes. The liver should be barely pink in the centre. Set aside to cool for 15 minutes.
3 Remove the thyme and bay leaf from the mixture and process in a food processor until smooth, then push through a sieve if you prefer an even smoother texture. Beat in the remaining butter using a wooden spoon, then add the brandy or port. Carefully fold in the cream or crème fraîche and season to taste with salt and freshly ground black pepper. Spoon into a serving bowl and serve with Melba toast or toasted bread fingers.

Chef's tip If prepared in advance and refrigerated, the pâté may be too firm to be eaten as a dip straight from the refrigerator. Allow to soften for about 30 minutes at room temperature before serving.

Salmon rillettes

This modern version of the classic French meat rillettes—similar to pâté—uses both fresh and smoked salmon.

*Preparation time **10 minutes + 1 hour chilling***
*Total cooking time **10 minutes***
*Serves **4 as an appetiser***

125 g (4 oz) salmon fillet, skinned and boned
60 g (2 oz) smoked salmon slices, finely chopped
80 g (2³/₄ oz) unsalted butter, at room temperature
60 ml (2 fl oz) natural yoghurt
1 teaspoon lemon juice
2 tablespoons chopped fresh chives

1 Steam the fresh salmon for 8–10 minutes, or until cooked through. Cool on a clean tea towel or several pieces of paper towel.
2 Using a whisk or fork, mix the smoked salmon with the butter until as smooth as possible. Add the yoghurt, lemon juice and chives. Mix until well combined, season to taste and set aside.
3 Gently crush the fresh salmon to make large flakes and add to the smoked salmon mixture. Mix until completely incorporated. Transfer to a small serving bowl or terrine and refrigerate for 1 hour, or until set. Serve with Melba toast or French bread.

Chef's tip You can also make a mackerel rillette by replacing the fresh salmon with three or four skinned and boned fresh mackerel fillets, about 125 g (4 oz). Replace the smoked salmon with the same quantity of smoked mackerel and substitute lime juice for the lemon juice.

Chicken liver pâté (top) and Salmon rillettes

Mini spring rolls

The mouthwatering combination of vegetables cooked with soy sauce, ginger, garlic and sesame seeds, enclosed in crisp golden brown filo pastry, makes these spring rolls a real treat. This recipe does not require a deep-fat fryer as the spring rolls are cooked in the oven.

Preparation time **40 minutes + 15 minutes cooling**
Total cooking time **15 minutes**
Makes **45**

**600 g (1 1/4 lb) mixed vegetables, such as leek,
carrot, swede, bean sprouts, snow peas
(mangetout) and celeriac**
1 tablespoon chopped spring onion
50 ml (1 3/4 fl oz) sesame oil
30 g (1 oz) fresh ginger, finely chopped
1 clove garlic, finely chopped
2 tablespoons sesame seeds, toasted (see Chef's tip)
1 tablespoon soy sauce
10 filo pastry sheets
150 g (5 oz) unsalted butter, melted

1 Brush two baking trays with a little melted butter and set aside.
2 Cut the peeled vegetables into long strips, about 2.5 mm (1/8 inch) thick, and combine with the spring onion. Heat the sesame oil in a shallow pan until smoking, then add the vegetables and spring onion and cook for 2 minutes, stirring continuously. Stir in the ginger, garlic, sesame seeds and soy sauce and cook for a

further 1 minute. Season to taste and turn the vegetable mixture out onto a plate or tray to cool completely.
3 Preheat the oven to moderately hot 200°C (400°F/Gas 6). Following the method in the Chef's techniques on page 63, lay a sheet of filo pastry on a work surface and brush one side with melted butter. Lay a second sheet on top of the buttered side and brush with more melted butter. Repeat to produce five double sheets, each with two layers of filo. Cut each double sheet into nine rectangles, each measuring about 9 x 15 cm (3 1/2 x 6 inches). Spoon an equal amount of filling onto the short end of each rectangle, leaving 1 cm (1/2 inch) free of filling on either side. Turn the sides in and roll up tightly to enclose the filling.
4 Place the rolls onto the prepared baking trays, brush with melted butter and bake in the oven for about 10–12 minutes, or until golden and crisp. Serve the spring rolls immediately, with some soy or sweet chilli sauce if desired.

Chef's tip To toast sesame seeds, place on a baking tray and bake in a moderate 180°C (350°F/Gas 4) oven for 4–5 minutes, or until golden brown. Alternatively, place them in a small frying pan and stir over medium heat until golden brown.

Onion tartlets

These delectable golden onion tartlets must be served warm. The onion filling can be replaced with a mushroom filling, as described in the chef's tip below. If short of time, you could use ready-made shortcrust pastry.

*Preparation time **45 minutes +35 minutes chilling***
*Total cooking time **45 minutes***
Makes 24

PASTRY
200 g (6¹/₂ oz) plain flour
¹/₄ teaspoon salt
40 g (1¹/₄ oz) unsalted butter, cut into cubes
2 egg yolks
4 tablespoons water

ONION FILLING
30 g (1 oz) unsalted butter
2 onions, finely chopped
1 small bay leaf
2 sprigs of fresh thyme

160 ml (5¹/₄ fl oz) thick (double) cream
4 eggs
4 egg yolks
pinch of ground nutmeg

1 Butter two 12-hole shallow patty pans or tart trays.
2 To make the pastry, sift together the flour and salt into a large bowl. Using your fingertips, rub in the cubed butter until the flour is evenly coloured and sandy in texture. Make a well in the centre and add the egg yolks and water. Mix well, form into a ball and cover with plastic wrap. Place in the refrigerator to chill for about 20 minutes.

3 To make the onion filling, melt the butter in a pan over medium heat. Add the onion, bay leaf and thyme with a pinch of salt. Cover and cook slowly for 15 minutes, then remove the cover and continue to cook for about 15 minutes, or until the onion is a dark golden colour. Remove the bay leaf and thyme and set aside to cool.

4 Roll out the dough to a thickness of 2 mm (¹/₈ inch), then refrigerate for 5 minutes. Preheat the oven to moderate 180°C (350°F/Gas 4). Using a round cutter, slightly larger than the holes in the patty pans, cut out 24 rounds. Place the rounds in each pan, pressing down on the bottom so that the dough extends slightly above the edge of the holes. Place in the refrigerator to chill for 10 minutes. Whisk together the cream, eggs, egg yolks, nutmeg and salt and freshly ground black pepper.

5 Divide the onion filling among the tartlet shells, then cover with the egg mixture. Bake for 12–15 minutes, or until lightly browned. Remove from the pans while still warm and serve immediately.

Chef's tip To replace the onion with a mushroom filling, melt 30 g (1 oz) butter in a saucepan over medium heat, add 3 finely chopped French shallots and cook for about 3 minutes. Toss 200 g (6¹/₂ oz) finely chopped mushrooms in 1 tablespoon lemon juice, add to the shallots and cook for another 10 minutes, or until dry. Set the filling aside to cool.

Pronto puff pizzas

Simply the quickest, crispiest and most moreish pizzas you'll ever make—these Pronto puffs are just ideal for the busy entertainer.

Preparation time **20 minutes**
Total cooking time **20 minutes**
Makes about 24

250 g (8 oz) block puff pastry
I egg, beaten
I small yellow capsicum (pepper)
I small red capsicum (pepper)
I zucchini (courgette), halved lengthways
2–3 tomatoes, sliced thinly
150 g (5 oz) artichoke hearts, drained and cut
   into I cm (1/2 inch) cubes
70 g (21/4 oz) mozzarella cheese, cut into
   I cm (1/2 inch) cubes
I teaspoon dried mixed herbs

1 Roll the pastry out on a floured work surface into a sheet about 3 mm (1/8 inch) thick. Place onto a baking tray and brush with the egg. Set aside in the refrigerator.
2 To grill the capsicums, follow the method in the Chef's techniques on page 62. Add the zucchini, skin-side-up, to the preheated grill a little after the capsicums, and also grill until the skin has blackened, but do not peel.
3 Preheat the oven to moderately hot 200°C (400°F/Gas 6). Slice the zucchini into 5 mm (1/4 inch) thick semicircles. Cut the peeled capsicums into 5 mm (1/4 inch) strips.
4 Using a 5 cm (2 inch) plain round cutter, cut circles from the pastry and place on two lightly greased baking trays. Top with a slice of tomato, a strip of yellow and red capsicum, some artichoke and zucchini, and a few cubes of mozzarella, then sprinkle lightly with the herbs. Bake in the oven for 8–10 minutes, or until puffed and lightly browned.

Spinach and feta parcels

*These delicious small parcels, resembling purses, have a lovely crisp exterior
and a soft creamy centre.*

*Preparation time **30 minutes + 15 minutes cooling***
*Total cooking time **20 minutes***
Makes about 45

75 g (2¹/₂ oz) unsalted butter, melted
1 tablespoon olive oil
250 g (8 oz) English spinach, torn
120 g (4 oz) feta cheese, crumbled with a fork
60 g (2 oz) ricotta or curd cheese
1 egg, beaten
1 tablespoon chopped fresh parsley
1 tablespoon chopped fresh basil
6 sheets filo pastry

1 Brush two baking trays with melted butter.
2 Heat the oil in a frying pan. Add the spinach and cook for 2 minutes, stirring continuously. Stir in the feta and ricotta until they become soft and coat the spinach.

Season to taste with salt and freshly ground black pepper. Remove the pan from the heat, cool slightly, then stir in the egg, parsley and basil. Set aside for about 15 minutes to cool completely.

3 Preheat the oven to moderately hot 190°C (375°F/ Gas 5). Following the method in the Chef's techniques on page 63, lay a sheet of filo pastry flat on a work surface and brush one side with melted butter. Lay a second sheet on top and brush with more melted butter. Repeat to produce three double sheets, each with two layers of filo. Cut each double sheet into 8 cm (3 inch) squares, discarding any leftover pastry. Put 1 teaspoon of filling in the centre of a square, then gather up the corners over the filling. Gently pinch the filo, just above the filling, to seal without splitting the pastry.

4 Place the parcels onto the prepared baking trays and drizzle with some of the remaining melted butter. Bake in the oven for about 15 minutes, or until crisp and golden brown.

Crudités

A colourful selection of crunchy fresh vegetables served with a choice of dipping sauces is an ideal summer dish for health-conscious guests.

Preparation time **35 minutes +**
1 hour chilling
Total cooking time **Nil**
Serves 8–10

SOUR CREAM DIP
250 ml (8 fl oz) sour cream
2 tablespoons mayonnaise
25 g (³/4 oz) Parmesan, grated
I teaspoon lime or lemon juice
¹/2 teaspoon Worcestershire sauce
I teaspoon horseradish sauce
¹/2 teaspoon Dijon mustard
¹/4 teaspoon celery salt

I long cucumber
2 sticks celery
I red capsicum (pepper)
I yellow capsicum (pepper)
I head broccoli
12 fresh baby corn
75 g (2¹/2 oz) snow peas (mangetout)
12 baby carrots
20 cherry tomatoes

HERB DIP
2 tablespoons Dijon mustard
4 tablespoons red wine vinegar
250 ml (8 fl oz) olive oil
¹/2 tablespoon each of chopped fresh chives, basil, parsley and tarragon

1 To prepare the sour cream dip, combine all the ingredients in a bowl and mix well. Chill for at least 1 hour before serving.

2 With a fork or a channelling knife, scrape down the length of the cucumber to create a ridged pattern, then cut into 5 mm (¹/4 inch) slices. Cut the celery and capsicums into 5–8 cm (2–3 inch) long sticks. Blanch the broccoli, corn, snow peas and carrots in boiling water for 1 minute. Drain, refresh in cold water and drain again. Remove the broccoli stem and discard. Cut the bushy green part into bite-sized pieces. Arrange all the vegetables on a serving platter. Cover with damp paper towels, then wrap in plastic wrap and refrigerate until ready to serve.

3 To prepare the herb dip, place the mustard in a bowl and whisk in the vinegar. Gradually whisk in the oil before adding the herbs and seasoning with salt and pepper. Serve the vegetables with the dips on the side.

Prawn gougères

Traditionally, a gougère is a round or ring-shaped cheese choux pastry. This variation uses plain choux pastry to make small puffs that are filled with a cold prawn and mayonnaise mixture.

Preparation time **40 minutes**
Total cooking time **25 minutes**
Makes about 20

50 g (1³/4 oz) unsalted butter, cut into small pieces
pinch of ground nutmeg
75 g (2¹/2 oz) plain flour
2 eggs, lightly beaten
1 beaten egg, for glazing
270 g (8³/4 oz) cooked and peeled prawns
  (see Chef's tip)
125 g (4 oz) mayonnaise
1 tablespoon finely chopped fresh chives

1 Preheat the oven to moderate 180°C (350°F/Gas 4) and lightly butter two baking trays.

2 To make the choux pastry, place 125 ml (4 fl oz) water, the butter, nutmeg and a pinch of salt in a saucepan and bring to the boil, then follow the method in the Chef's techniques on page 63.

3 Spoon the choux pastry into a piping bag fitted with a small plain nozzle. Pipe out small balls of dough the size of walnuts onto the prepared baking trays, leaving a space of 3 cm (1¹/4 inches) between each ball. Lightly brush the top of each ball with the beaten egg, being careful not to let any excess egg drip down onto the baking tray, as this may prevent the balls from rising evenly. Bake in the oven for 30 minutes, or until the balls have puffed up and are golden brown. Remove from the oven and transfer to a wire rack to cool.

4 Roughly chop the prawns and place in a bowl, then add the mayonnaise and chopped chives and mix together. Season to taste with salt and freshly ground black pepper. Refrigerate until ready to use.

5 Once the choux balls have cooled, cut in half and remove any soft dough from inside the balls. Fill each ball with a small spoonful of the prawn mixture. Replace the tops, arrange on a serving platter and serve.

Chef's tip If purchasing unpeeled prawns, you will need to buy about 640 g (1 lb 4¹/2 oz).

Minted pea and coriander triangles

Despite being a little time consuming to prepare, the advantage of these tasty savouries is that they can be made in advance and baked in the oven as required. It is worth noting that they are suitable for vegetarians.

Preparation time **55 minutes + 20 minutes cooling**
Total cooking time **30 minutes**
Makes 30

sprig of fresh mint
175 g (5³/4 oz) peas
I tablespoon vegetable oil
I onion, cut into cubes the same size as the peas
2 potatoes, about 150 g (5 oz), cooked and mashed
2 teaspoons ground coriander
I tablespoon chopped fresh coriander
I tablespoon finely chopped fresh mint
I tablespoon lemon juice, to taste
6 sheets filo pastry
60 g (2 oz) unsalted butter, melted

1 Place the sprig of mint into a pan of salted water and bring to the boil. When boiling, add the peas and cook for 2 minutes. Pour into a colander to drain, then remove and discard the mint.

2 Heat the oil in a frying pan over low heat, add the onion and cook for 7 minutes, or until soft and translucent. Increase the heat to medium, add the peas and potato and stir to combine. Transfer to a small bowl and set aside for about 20 minutes to cool.

3 When cool, stir in the ground and fresh coriander, the chopped mint and lemon juice, then season to taste with salt and black pepper. Preheat the oven to moderately hot 190°C (375°F/Gas 5). Brush two baking trays with some melted butter.

4 Lay the sheets of filo pastry out on a work surface and brush with the melted butter. Cut across each sheet to form five strips, about 8 cm (3 inches) wide. Place 2 teaspoons of the filling on the corner of one end of each strip. Fold the pastry over diagonally to form a triangle at the end. Then keep on folding diagonally until you have reached the other end of the strip.

5 Place the triangles onto the prepared trays, brush with a little melted butter and bake for 15 minutes, or until crisp and golden brown.

Chef's tip These triangles can be prepared a day in advance and refrigerated before baking.

Crab fritters with a lime and yoghurt mayonnaise

Warm crab and herb fritters are served here with a light tangy dipping sauce. The yoghurt and lime in the sauce provide a refreshing contrast to the richness of the mayonnaise.

Preparation time **20 minutes**
Total cooking **15 minutes**
Makes about 30

LIME AND YOGHURT MAYONNAISE
2 teaspoons grated lime rind
125 g (4 oz) natural yoghurt
125 g (4 oz) mayonnaise
fresh lime juice, to taste

CRAB FRITTERS
250 g (8 oz) skinned white fish fillets, such as whiting, sole or haddock
1 egg white
60 ml (2 fl oz) thick (double) cream
250 g (8 oz) cooked white crab meat
2 tablespoons chopped mixed fresh herbs, such as dill, chives, parsley and tarragon
250 g (8 oz) fresh breadcrumbs

oil, for deep-frying

1 To make the lime and yoghurt mayonnaise, stir the lime rind into the yoghurt. Mix in the mayonnaise and lime juice to taste, then season with salt and freshly ground black pepper. Cover with plastic wrap and set aside in the refrigerator.

2 To make the crab fritters, purée the fish fillets in a food processor. Add the egg white and some salt and pepper and process again until well blended. Using the pulse button on the processor, carefully add the cream. Do not overwork or the cream will separate. Transfer the mixture to a large bowl and set inside another bowl of ice. Using a large metal spoon or plastic spatula, fold in the crab meat and mixed herbs. Using two teaspoons, shape the mixture into small ovals, or roll by hand into round balls, about 3 cm (1¹/4 inches) in diameter. Sprinkle the breadcrumbs on to a sheet of paper and roll the balls in them to coat each one, using the paper to help attach the crumbs without handling the soft mixture too much.

3 Deep-fry the fritters for 4–6 minutes, following the method in the Chef's techniques on page 63. Season the fritters with salt and serve warm with the lime and yoghurt mayonnaise on the side.

Chef's tip Once shaped and coated, the crab fritters can be covered with plastic wrap and refrigerated for up to 24 hours before frying.

Cranberry chicken cups

Delicate, creamy little mouthfuls, quick to prepare and guaranteed to impress.

Preparation time **20 minutes**
Total cooking time **10 minutes**
Makes **26**

6 sheets filo pastry
150 g (5 oz) unsalted butter, melted
3 cooked skinless chicken breast fillets, cut into
**   1 cm (1/2 inch) cubes**
1 tablespoon cranberry sauce
3 tablespoons crème fraîche
2 spring onions, finely chopped
1/2 teaspoon finely grated lemon rind
fresh coriander leaves, to garnish
thin strips of lemon rind, to garnish

1 Preheat the oven to moderately hot 200°C (400°F/Gas 6). Following the method in the Chef's techniques on page 63, lay a sheet of filo out on a work surface and brush with the butter. Place a second sheet on top and brush with butter, then repeat to make three layers. Do the same with the remaining filo.
2 Using a round 7 cm (2³/4 inch) cutter, cut 26 discs from the filo and, buttered-side-down, press gently into individual fluted tartlet tins, 5 cm (2 inches) across and 2 cm (³/4 inch) deep, or patty pans.
3 Place small circles of greaseproof paper into the pastry cases and fill with baking beans or rice. Bake for 10 minutes, or until golden. Remove the rice or beans and cool the pastry in the tins.
4 In a bowl, combine the chicken, cranberry sauce, crème fraîche, spring onion, lemon rind and some salt and pepper. Spoon into the tartlet cases and garnish with a coriander leaf and the lemon rind.

Chef's tip The chicken can be replaced with cooked turkey, duck or flaked smoked trout.

Smoked salmon and trout roulade on pumpernickel

Pumpernickel, a coarse, dark bread made from a high proportion of rye flour, has a slightly sour taste, which complements the rich creamy taste of the smoked fish topping.

*Preparation time **25 minutes + 30 minutes chilling***
*Total cooking time **Nil***
*Makes **20***

100 g (3¼ oz) smoked trout fillet
100 g (3¼ oz) cream cheese
1 tablespoon lemon juice
200 g (6½ oz) smoked salmon slices
200 g (6½ oz) pumpernickel, sliced
sprigs of fresh chervil or parsley, to garnish

1 Remove any skin or bones from the trout and place into a food processor with 85 g (2¾ oz) of the cream cheese. Process until blended and smooth, then season to taste with salt and pepper. Add the lemon juice and process once more to combine.

2 Lay the smoked salmon slices onto a piece of plastic wrap in a 15 x 20 cm (6 x 8 inch) rectangular shape, with the edges of the slices overlapping. Spread an even layer of the smoked trout mixture onto the salmon, then roll the slices up from the widest side, using the plastic wrap to help lift as you roll. Wrap the salmon and trout roulade in plastic wrap and place it in the freezer for 30 minutes, or until set and firm enough to slice.

3 Using a 4.5 cm (1¾ inch) cutter, cut 20 rounds from the pumpernickel. Spread the remaining cream cheese on to the pumpernickel circles. Remove the salmon roulade from the freezer, discard the plastic wrap and cut across the roulade, using a very sharp knife, to make about 20 slices. Top each piece of pumpernickel with a roulade slice and decorate with a sprig of chervil or parsley. Cover with plastic wrap and keep chilled until ready to serve.

Creamed Roquefort and walnuts

These delicious easily prepared toasts are best made less than 30 minutes in advance to avoid the toast from becoming too soft.

*Preparation time **15 minutes***
*Total cooking time **10 minutes***
Makes 40

25 g (³/4 oz) walnuts, roughly chopped
10 slices wholegrain bread, about 5 mm
  (¹/4 inch) thick
60 g (2 oz) Roquefort or other strong blue cheese
60 g (2 oz) cream cheese
chopped fresh parsley, to garnish

1 Spread the walnuts on to a baking tray and toast them under a preheated grill for 3–5 minutes, shaking the tray frequently to ensure that they are evenly browned and do not burn. Alternatively, toast the nuts for 7–10 minutes in a moderate oven at 180°C (350°F/Gas 4). Set aside to cool.

2 Cut the bread slices into 4 cm (1¹/2 inch) circles using a plain round cutter. Toast lightly on both sides using the grill, then set aside.

3 In a small bowl, break up the Roquefort using a fork, add the cream cheese and mix well. Stir in half the walnuts, then spread the mixture on to each round of toast. Sprinkle the remaining chopped walnuts and some parsley on to the cheese mixture to decorate.

Crostini of roasted capsicum and basil

The name crostini comes from the Italian word 'crosta', meaning 'crust'. Crostini are small rounds of toasted bread with toppings such as pâté, cheese or, as in this case, roasted vegetables.

*Preparation time **25 minutes***
*Total cooking time **10 minutes***
Makes 12

¹/2 small red capsicum (pepper), sliced in half
¹/2 small green capsicum (pepper), sliced in half
2 tablespoons shredded fresh basil
70 ml (2¹/4 fl oz) olive oil
¹/2 baguette (preferably stale)
1 clove garlic
Parmesan shavings, to garnish

1 Preheat the oven to moderately hot 200°C (400°F/Gas 6). To grill the capsicums, follow the method in the Chef's techniques on page 62.

2 Cut the capsicums into thin strips and put them into a bowl with the basil and 1 tablespoon of the olive oil, or just enough to bind the mixture. Season with salt and freshly ground black pepper

3 Cut the baguette into slices 1.5 cm (⁵/8 inch) thick. Toast the slices on both sides under a preheated grill or in a toaster, then brush them with the remaining oil. Rub the garlic clove over the crostini and spoon some of the roasted capsicum mixture onto each one. Serve immediately, topped with the Parmesan shavings.

Mini blinis with caviar

Brightly coloured and extremely appetising, these small pancakes topped with sour cream and caviar or roe are bound to disappear very quickly.

Preparation time **45 minutes + 30 minutes resting**
Total cooking time **35 minutes**
Makes 40–45

10 g (¹/4 oz) fresh yeast or 5 g (¹/8 oz) dried yeast
155 ml (5 fl oz) milk, lukewarm
2 teaspoons sugar
70 g (2¹/4 oz) plain flour
50 g (1³/4 oz) buckwheat flour
2 eggs, separted
40 g (1¹/4 oz) butter, melted but cooled
sour cream, to garnish
caviar or lumpfish roe, to garnish
sprigs of fresh dill or chervil, to garnish

1 Dissolve the yeast in the lukewarm milk, then mix in the sugar, flours, egg yolks and a large pinch of salt. Cover and set aside to rest for 30 minutes in a warm place. After resting, the batter should be foamy and thick. Mix in the melted butter.

2 Beat the egg whites with a pinch of salt until soft peaks form. Gently fold into the batter.

3 Over medium heat, melt a little butter in a non-stick frying pan. Using a small spoon, place dollops of the batter in the pan, trying to make them as uniform as possible and being careful not to overcrowd them. Once the batter begins to set around the edges and the surface is bubbly, carefully flip the blinis over. Cook for another 2–3 minutes, or until brown. Transfer to a wire rack to cool (you can overlap them, but do not stack). Repeat until all the batter has been used.

4 If necessary, use a small round cutter to trim the blinis to the same size. Arrange on a serving platter and place a spoon of sour cream in the centre and top with some caviar or roe. Finish with a sprig of dill or chervil.

Chef's tip If you have any fresh yeast left over, it can be stored in the refrigerator, lightly wrapped in greaseproof paper, for up to 2 weeks.

Potato and smoked fish croquettes

Deliciously crisp, golden brown potato croquettes flavoured with smoked fish and garlic, which can be served with the sauce of your choice, whether a tomato sauce, garlic mayonnaise or salsa.

Preparation time **30 minutes + 15 minutes chilling**
Total cooking time **45 minutes**
Makes 40

500 g (1 lb) floury potatoes, such as King Edward
20 g (3/4 oz) unsalted butter
1 egg yolk
pinch of ground nutmeg
1 tablespoon olive oil
2 cloves garlic, crushed
100 ml (31/4 fl oz) thick (double) cream
150 g (5 oz) smoked haddock, trout or salmon,
** crumbled or thinly sliced**
60 g (2 oz) plain flour
3 eggs, beaten
1 tablespoon peanut (groundnut) oil
150 g (5 oz) fresh breadcrumbs
oil, for deep-frying

1 Cut the peeled potatoes into equal-size pieces for even cooking. Place them in a medium saucepan, cover with cold water and add a large pinch of salt. Bring to the boil, lower the heat and simmer for at least 20 minutes, or until they are quite tender.

2 Drain the potatoes and dry them by shaking them in their pan over a low heat. Press them through a sieve or finely mash and add the butter, egg yolk, nutmeg and some salt and pepper. Place the mixture into a large bowl to cool.

3 Heat the olive oil in a saucepan, add the garlic and cook for 1 minute to soften. Stir in the cream and reduce by half. Add the fish to the potato mixture with the reduced cream. Season with salt and pepper and mix to combine well.

4 Season the flour with salt and pepper and place in a shallow tray. Place the beaten egg and peanut oil into a shallow bowl and the breadcrumbs on to a large piece of greaseproof paper. Shape the potato mixture into ovals about 2 x 4 cm (3/4 x 11/2 inches) in size and roll each one carefully in the flour, patting off the excess. Dip them in the egg, then drain off the excess and roll them in the breadcrumbs, lifting the edges of the paper to help you. Sometimes it is necessary to coat the croquettes twice in the egg and breadcrumbs, especially if your mixture is a little too soft to hold its shape well. Refrigerate for 15 minutes.

5 Heat the oil in a deep-fat fryer or deep saucepan (see Chef's techniques, page 63). Deep-fry, in batches, for 3–4 minutes, or until golden brown. Lift out, draining off excess oil, and drain on crumpled paper towels. Serve the croquettes with a sauce and lime wedges.

Chef's tip The potato must not be too wet or the moisture will cause the croquettes to split and absorb the oil. Using breadcrumbs on a large piece of paper enables you to coat the croquettes without too much mess. Always shake off or press on excess breadcrumbs or they will fall into the oil when frying, burn and then cling to the croquettes as unsightly specks.

Smoked salmon pancake rolls

One of the attractive features of this recipe, which successfully combines the flavours of smoked salmon and horseradish, is that the pancakes may be prepared in advance and frozen

*Preparation time **1 hour + 15 minutes resting +***
   1 hour refrigeration
*Total cooking time **10 minutes***
Makes 30–35

PANCAKE DOUGH
125 g (4 oz) plain flour
2 teaspoons sesame oil

150 g (5 oz) cream cheese, at room temperature
1 tablespoon horseradish cream
1/2 teaspoon lemon juice
200 g (6 1/2 oz) smoked salmon slices
chopped fresh chives or herbs, to garnish

1 To make the pancake dough, bring 90 ml (3 fl oz) water to the boil, and follow the method for preparing pancakes in the Chef's techniques on page 62. Stack the pancakes on a plate and keep them wrapped in a slightly damp cloth to prevent them from drying out.

2 Soften the cream cheese in a small bowl and mix with the horseradish and lemon juice until smooth.

3 Place a pancake on a work surface and trim off the upper third of the circle. Spread with a thin layer of the cheese mixture, then cover with a layer of salmon. Roll up as tightly as possible. Wrap in plastic wrap to keep it from unrolling and set aside. Repeat with the remaining pancakes. Refrigerate for at least 1 hour.

4 Just before serving, trim the ends of each roll, then slice into 1.5 cm (5/8 inch) pieces and pierce with a cocktail stick. Scatter a few chives or fresh herbs in the centre of each roll, arrange on a platter and serve.

Chef's tip The pancakes may be prepared ahead of time and frozen. Briefly steam to soften before using.

Blue cheese puffs

Any type of blue cheese, such as Stilton or the creamy Italian Dolcelatte, may be used to make these puffs. However, if you use the strong salty Roquefort cheese, omit the salt in the recipe.

*Preparation time **10 minutes***
*Total cooking time **25 minutes***
Makes about 55

CHOUX PASTRY
100 g (3¹/4 oz) unsalted butter
100 g (3¹/4 oz) strong or plain flour
2 eggs, beaten

100 g (3¹/4 oz) blue cheese, grated
pinch of dry mustard, optional
oil, for deep-frying
finely chopped fresh chives, to garnish

1 To make the choux pastry, melt the butter and 200 ml (6¹/2 fl oz) water in a large pan over low heat, then follow the method in the Chef's techniques on page 63. Stir in the cheese and season to taste with salt, pepper and the mustard if desired.

2 Heat the oil in a deep-fat fryer or deep saucepan (see Chef's techniques, page 63). Using two lightly oiled teaspoons, scoop out a small amount of the mixture with one and push off with the other spoon to carefully lower into the hot oil. Cook the mixture in batches until puffed, golden brown and crisp, turning with a long-handled metal spoon to ensure even colouring. Drain on crumpled paper towels.

3 Sprinkle the warm puffs lightly with the chives and serve immediately.

Chef's tip The puff mixture may be prepared in advance, covered with plastic wrap and refrigerated for a few hours before deep-frying.

Corn and chicken fritters

Golden kernels of juicy sweet corn with the distinctive flavour of coriander and soy sauce make these fritters irresistible.

Preparation time **20 minutes + refrigeration**
Total cooking time **45 minutes**
Makes about 65

2 eggs, lightly beaten
2 x 420 g (13 1/4 oz) cans sweet corn, well drained
30 g (1 oz) cornflour
400 g (12 3/4 oz) skinless chicken breast fillet,
 finely chopped
2 tablespoons chopped fresh coriander
1 tablespoon caster sugar
1 tablespoon soy sauce
oil, for frying

1 In a large bowl, combine the eggs, sweet corn, cornflour, chicken, coriander, sugar and soy sauce and mix well. Cover and leave to chill in the refrigerator for at least 1 hour, or overnight if possible.

2 In a large frying pan, heat a 3 mm (1/8 inch) depth of oil. Using a tablespoon, drop in enough sweet corn mixture to make 3 cm (1 1/4 inch) circles, taking care not to overcrowd the pan. Fry for 3 minutes, or until golden, then turn over to brown the second side. Lift out and drain on crumpled paper towels. Repeat with the remaining mixture, adding more oil to the pan when necessary. Serve the fritters warm.

Chef's tips Make the first fritter a small one, taste to check the seasoning and, if necessary, add salt and pepper to the mixture before cooking the rest.

 These fritters are delicious topped with some natural yoghurt and a drizzle of sweet chilli sauce.

Cheese palmiers

These small savouries are delicious served with a cocktail or to accompany a soup. They can either be made as palmiers or as cheese straws.

*Preparation time **30 minutes + 45 minutes refrigeration***
*Total cooking time **10 minutes***
Makes 40

2 egg yolks
I egg
1/4 teaspoon caster sugar
80 g (23/4 oz) Parmesan, grated
1/2 teaspoon paprika
375 g (12 oz) block puff pastry

1 Beat together the egg yolks, egg, sugar and about 1/4 teaspoon salt and strain into a clean bowl.

2 Brush two baking trays with melted butter and place in the refrigerator. In a bowl, combine the Parmesan, paprika, 1/2 teaspoon salt and some black pepper.

3 Divide the pastry in two and on a lightly floured surface, roll each piece into a 30 x 15 cm (12 x 6 inch) rectangle, about 3 mm (1/8 inch) thick. Brush lightly with the egg and sprinkle with the Parmesan mixture. Roll over the Parmesan with a rolling pin to press it into the pastry, then carefully slide the pastry sheets onto two trays and refrigerate for 15 minutes.

4 Transfer the pastry sheets to a lightly floured surface and trim back to 30 x 15 cm (12 x 6 inch) rectangles.

With the back of a knife, lightly mark six 5 cm (2 inch) strips on each sheet, parallel with the shortest side. Sprinkle with a little water.

5 Fold the two outer strips of each sheet inwards. Their non-cheese undersides will now be on the top. Brush with a little water and fold over onto the next marked strips, brush with water again and fold onto each other. Transfer to a tray and chill for 15 minutes. Cut into 5 mm (1/4 inch) slices and place, cut-side-down and well apart, on the prepared baking trays. Press down to lightly flatten, turn over and chill for 15 minutes.

6 Meanwhile, preheat the oven to moderately hot 200°C (400°F/Gas 6). Bake the palmiers for 8 minutes, or until golden and crisp. Remove to a wire rack to cool.

Chef's tips As a variation, you could add some dried mixed herbs, finely chopped sun-dried tomato or anchovy to the cheese.

To make cheese straws, use the same ingredients and follow the method for steps 1–3. Cut 1 cm (1/2 inch) wide strips from the pastry sheets and twist each several times to form a long, loose ringlet. Place on the baking trays and press both ends down firmly. Chill for about 15 minutes, then bake for 12–15 minutes, or until golden and crisp. Immediately cut each straw into 10 cm (4 inch) lengths and remove to a wire rack to cool.

Roquefort in witlof leaves

The butter used in this recipe helps to soften both the texture and the distinctive salty taste of the Roquefort, a blue-vein ewe's milk cheese from southern France.

Preparation time **20 minutes**
Total cooking time **Nil**
Makes 40–45

260 g (8¼ oz) Roquefort or other strong blue cheese
140 g (4½ oz) unsalted butter, at room temperature
I tablespoon port
4 witlof (chicory)
2 tablespoons chopped walnuts
a few sprigs of fresh parsley, to garnish

1 Place the cheese, butter and port in a food processor and process until smooth. Season to taste with freshly ground black pepper and more port if desired. Transfer to a bowl and set aside.

2 Remove any damaged outer leaves from the witlof and discard. Cut about 5 mm (¼ inch) from the bottom and carefully remove all the loose leaves. Repeat until all the leaves are loose.

3 Put the cheese mixture into a piping bag fitted with a medium star nozzle and pipe a small rosette of cheese at the bottom of each witlof leaf. Sprinkle with some chopped walnuts, then arrange on a round platter with the tips of the witlof leaves pointing outward like the petals of a flower. Form the parsley into a bouquet and place in the centre. Serve immediately.

Chef's tip The cheese filling may be prepared ahead of time and stored, covered with plastic wrap, in the refrigerator, but once the witlof is cut it tends to discolour, so prepare the leaves just before serving.

Spiced prawn balls

The fried sesame seeds enclosing the tasty prawn mixture will give a strong, distinctive flavour and a lovely golden brown colour to these delicious savoury snacks.

Preparation time **15 minutes + 20 minutes chilling**
Total cooking time **15 minutes**
Makes 24

750 g (1¹/2 lb) large raw prawns
1 tablespoon oil
2 cloves garlic, crushed
1 cm (¹/2 inch) fresh ginger, chopped finely
¹/4 teaspoon salt
2 teaspoons sugar
1 teaspoon chopped fresh coriander
1 teaspoon cornflour
¹/2 egg white
100 g (3¹/4 oz) sesame seeds
oil, for deep-frying

1 Remove the shells from the prawns. Take each prawn and make a shallow cut along the back with a small knife, then carefully pull out the dark vein with the tip of the knife. Pat dry with paper towels.

2 Put the prawns in a food processor and process to a coarse purée. Transfer to a bowl and add the oil, garlic, ginger, salt, sugar, coriander and cornflour and mix well to combine.

3 Lightly whisk the egg white until it just stands in soft peaks, then add just enough of the egg white to the spiced prawn mixture to obtain a smooth, stiff but shapable mixture.

4 Divide the mixture into 24 evenly sized balls. Roll them in the sesame seeds to coat, set them on a baking tray and chill in the refrigerator for 20 minutes.

5 Heat the oil in a deep-fat fryer or deep saucepan (see Chef's techniques, page 63). Cook the balls in three batches, for about 4–5 minutes, or until they are golden brown and crispy on the outside and cooked through. Drain on crumpled paper towels. Arrange them on a serving plate and serve hot.

Cornish pasties

In the eighteenth and nineteenth centuries, Cornish pasties were taken down the mines by miners and eaten as a complete meal. There was meat at one end and apple or jam at the other, with scrolled initials in the pastry to indicate the difference. This recipe, however, is for modern savoury pasties that have been miniaturised and adapted to be served as finger food.

Preparation time **35 minutes + 30 minutes chilling**
Total cooking time **30 minutes**
Makes 48

PASTRY
500 g (1 lb) plain flour
pinch of salt
200 g (6¹/₂ oz) unsalted butter, cut into
    cubes and chilled
50 g (1³/₄ oz) lard, cut into cubes and chilled
6–8 tablespoons water

FILLING
1 potato, about 80 g (2³/₄ oz), roughly chopped
¹/₄ swede, about 100 g (3¹/₄ oz), roughly chopped
15 g (¹/₂ oz) unsalted butter
¹/₂ onion, finely chopped
125 g (4 oz) lean minced beef
50 g (1³/₄ oz) kidneys, finely chopped, optional

milk, for brushing

1 To make the pastry, sift the flour and salt into a large bowl and add the butter and lard. Using a fast, light, flicking action of thumb across fingertips, rub the butter and lard into the flour until the mixture resembles fine breadcrumbs. Make a well, add 1 tablespoon of the water and mix with a round-bladed knife until small lumps form. Continue to add the tablespoons of water, making a different well for each one and only using the last tablespoon if necessary. When the mixture is in large lumps, pick up and lightly pull together. Knead the pastry on a lightly floured surface until just smooth. Wrap in plastic wrap and chill in the refrigerator for 20 minutes. Brush two baking trays with melted butter and set aside.

2 To make the filling, put the potato and swede into a food processor and, using the pulse button, finely chop but do not purée. Melt the butter in a frying pan, add the onion and cook gently for 4 minutes. Add the potato and swede, turn the heat up to medium and cook for about 2 minutes, stirring occasionally, until just tender. Add the beef and kidney, turn the heat to high and fry, stirring continuously, for 5 minutes. Drain off the excess fat, season well with salt and pepper and leave to cool.

3 Cut the pastry in two and on a lightly floured surface, roll out the sheets to a 2 mm (¹/₈ inch) thickness. Cut out about 24 circles, using a 6 cm (2¹/₂ inch) round cutter, from each sheet of pastry, and place 1 teaspoon of the filling on one side, 5 mm (¹/₄ inch) from the edge. Moisten the edge with water and fold the unfilled side over to form a semicircle, pressing the edges together well to seal. Using a fork, press down on the edge of the pastries to form a decorative pattern. With the point of a knife, twist to make a small steam vent on top of each pastry and lay them on the prepared trays. Place in the refrigerator to chill for 10 minutes.

4 Preheat the oven to moderately hot 200°C (400°F/Gas 6). Brush the top of the pasties with a little milk and bake in the oven for 15 minutes, or until the pasties are golden brown.

Satay beef sticks

Widely cooked throughout Southeast Asia, a satay consists of marinated meat, fish or poultry, threaded onto bamboo or wooden skewers, grilled, and served with a sauce.

Preparation time **35 minutes + 2–3 hours marinating**
Total cooking time **15 minutes**
Makes 20

¹/4 teaspoon ground aniseed
¹/4 teaspoon ground cumin
I teaspoon ground turmeric
I teaspoon ground coriander
I French shallot, chopped
I clove garlic, finely chopped
1.5 cm (⁵/8 inch) piece of fresh ginger, finely chopped
I stalk lemon grass, white part only, finely chopped
I tablespoon brown sugar
35 ml (1¹/4 fl oz) peanut (groundnut) oil
I teaspoon soy sauce
200 g (6¹/2 oz) beef fillet or sirloin, cut into 20 thin strips

SATAY SAUCE
I clove garlic
80 g (2³/4 oz) smooth peanut butter
40 ml (1¹/4 fl oz) coconut milk
a few drops of Tabasco, or to taste
2 teaspoons honey
2 teaspoons lemon juice
2 teaspoons light soy sauce

1 Soak 20 short wooden skewers in water for 1 hour to prevent them burning under the grill. To make the marinade, add the ground aniseed, cumin, turmeric and coriander to the shallot, garlic, ginger, lemon grass and brown sugar in a medium bowl. Mix well and add the oil and soy sauce.

2 Thread a strip of beef onto each wooden skewer (see Chef's techniques, page 62) and place in a shallow dish. Thoroughly coat in the marinade and refrigerate for 2–3 hours.

3 To make the satay sauce, put the garlic into a small pan and cover with cold water. Bring to the boil and simmer for 3 minutes, refresh under cold water, then drain and finely chop. Combine the garlic with the peanut butter, coconut milk and 60 ml (2 fl oz) water in a medium saucepan. Stir over medium heat for 1–2 minutes, or until smooth and thick, then add the Tabasco, honey, lemon juice and soy sauce. Stir until the sauce is warm and thoroughly blended. If the mixture starts to separate, stir in 1–2 teaspoons water. Cover with plastic wrap and place in the refrigerator until ready to use.

4 Preheat a grill or barbecue until hot. Cook the beef satay sticks for 1–2 minutes on each side, turning three or four times during cooking. Once they are cooked, arrange on a plate and serve with the satay sauce.

Welsh rarebit

Originally called Welsh rabbit, the name of these toasted cheese slices was changed to Welsh rarebit in the eighteenth century. It has been speculated that rarebit was originally 'rearbit', because these treats were served at the end of a meal.

Preparation time **15 minutes**
Total cooking time **4 minutes**
Makes 16

60 g (2 oz) Gruyère cheese, grated
60 g (2 oz) Cheddar, grated
1 teaspoon French mustard
pinch of cayenne pepper
1 egg, beaten
1 tablespoon beer
4 slices bread
15 g (¹/₂ oz) unsalted butter, at room temperature
chopped fresh parsley, to garnish

1 Preheat the grill. Mix the Gruyère and Cheddar together, stir in the mustard and cayenne pepper and season with salt and black pepper. Mix in the beaten egg and beer and set aside.

2 Remove the crusts from the bread and toast the slices on both sides. Immediately spread one side of each slice with the butter. Spoon the cheese mixture on to the toast and spread neatly, making sure that all the edges are covered.

3 Place under the grill for 3–4 minutes, or until the cheese mixture is bubbling and lightly browned. Remove and immediately cut each slice into four fingers or triangles. Sprinkle with the chopped parsley and serve hot.

Prawn toast

These are quick and easy to prepare and can be cut to any shape. They must be served warm.

Preparation time **20 minutes + 30 minutes refrigeration**
Total cooking time **15 minutes**
Makes about 40

12 peeled and deveined large raw prawns, about 360 g (11¹/₂ oz)
2 teaspoons sherry
¹/₂ teaspoon salt
¹/₂ teaspoon pepper
2 teaspoons sesame oil
2 egg whites
2 tablespoons cornflour
1¹/₂ tablespoons chopped fresh coriander
2 spring onions, finely chopped
10 slices sandwich bread
whole fresh coriander leaves, to garnish
oil, for deep-frying

1 In a food processor, process the prawns until finely chopped. Add the sherry, salt, pepper, sesame oil, egg whites and cornflour. Process until smooth, then stir in the chopped coriander and spring onion.

2 Remove the crusts from the bread slices. Spread on a layer of prawn purée, half the thickness of the bread, all the way to the edges. Refrigerate for 30 minutes, or until the purée is firm. Cut the bread into squares, triangles or rectangles and smooth the cut edges if necessary. Press a coriander leaf on to each shape.

3 Heat the oil in a deep-fat fryer or deep saucepan (see Chef's techniques, page 63). Deep-fry the prawn toasts in batches for 2–3 minutes, or until golden brown. Remove with a slotted spoon and drain on crumpled paper towels. Serve immediately.

Welsh rarebit (top) and Prawn toast

Melting morsels

As the name suggests, these rich cheese biscuits melt in the mouth. They may be prepared up to a week in advance as they keep well if stored in an airtight container in a cool place.

Preparation time **35 minutes + 50 minutes chilling**
Total cooking time **10 minutes per tray**
Makes **64**

90 g (3 oz) plain flour
pinch of celery salt
90 g (3 oz) unsalted butter, cut into cubes and chilled
75 g (2¹/2 oz) Cheddar, grated
15 g (¹/2 oz) Parmesan, grated
I egg yolk
I egg, beaten
10 g (¹/4 oz) Parmesan, finely grated, for the topping

1 Preheat the oven to moderately hot 190°C (375°F/Gas 5). Brush two baking trays with melted butter and refrigerate.

2 Sift the flour, celery salt and a pinch of salt and freshly ground black pepper together into a medium bowl. Add the butter cubes and, using two round-bladed knives, cut the mixture from the centre to the edges of the bowl with a quick action.

3 When the flour has almost disappeared into the butter, add the Cheddar and Parmesan and continue cutting for a few moments more until the mixture is blended and coming together in rough lumps. Make a well in the centre and cut in the egg yolk until combined. Gather together by hand to form a ball.

4 Wrap the dough loosely in plastic wrap and flatten slightly. Chill for about 20 minutes until firm.

5 Place the dough on a lightly floured work surface. Cut in half and roll out each half to a 20 cm (8 inch) square, 4 mm (¹/4 inch) thick. Cut each square into 16 small squares, then cut each square in half to form triangles. Using a palette knife, carefully place on enough triangles to comfortably fill the two baking trays, and chill for 30 minutes.

6 Brush each biscuit with beaten egg and sprinkle with a pinch of the extra Parmesan. Bake for 10 minutes, or until golden brown. Place on a wire rack to cool. Repeat with the remaining mixture, preparing the trays as instructed in step 1.

Chef's tip Try varying the topping by sprinkling with finely chopped nuts and rock salt, poppy seeds or Parmesan mixed with a pinch of cayenne.

Mini brochettes

It is important to marinate the ingredients as this will bring more flavour to the brochettes and make sure that the meat is deliciously tender.

Preparation time **25 minutes + 1 hour marinating**
Total cooking time **15 minutes**
Makes 20

180 ml (5³/4 fl oz) veal or chicken stock
2 cloves garlic, crushed
2 teaspoons chopped fresh ginger
2 tablespoons dark soy sauce
2 teaspoons sesame oil
1 skinless chicken breast fillet, cut into 1 cm (¹/2 inch)
  cubes
¹/2 red capsicum (pepper), cut into 1 cm
  (¹/2 inch) cubes
¹/2 yellow capsicum (pepper), cut into 1 cm
  (¹/2 inch) cubes
2 spring onions, sliced diagonally
1 teaspoon cornflour

1   Soak 20 short wooden skewers in water for 1 hour to prevent them scorching under the grill. Pour the stock into a pan and simmer until it has reduced by a third and is syrupy. In a bowl, combine the reduced stock with the garlic, ginger, soy and sesame oil. Leave to cool.
2   Thread alternating pieces of chicken, red and yellow capsicum and spring onion onto the skewers. Place the brochettes in a flat dish and season. Pour half the cooled marinade over the brochettes. Cover with plastic wrap and refrigerate for at least 1 hour.
3 To make the dipping sauce, heat the remaining marinade in a small pan, then mix the cornflour with a little water and stir in until the sauce boils and thickens. Set aside and keep warm.
4 Preheat the grill. Drain the brochettes and cook under the grill for 3 minutes, turning, until the meat is cooked. Serve immediately with the dipping sauce.

Parma ham and melon fingers

An extremely refreshing all-time favourite that is best made with paper-thin slices of Parma ham or prosciutto.

Preparation time **10 minutes**
Total cooking time **Nil**
Makes 32

I small melon
II slices Parma ham or prosciutto

1 Cut the melon in half lengthways and, using a spoon, remove the seeds and gently scrape clean. Slice each half into eight wedges.
2 With a sharp knife, starting at one end of a melon wedge, slice between the flesh and the thick skin of the melon. Cut each piece of peeled melon in half.
3 Cut each slice of Parma ham or prosciutto into three long strips.
4 Wrap a strip of Parma ham or prosciutto around each wedge of melon and secure with a cocktail stick.

Red mullet and tapenade on toast

Tapenade, a simple spread from Provence in France, is made by puréeing black olives, anchovies, capers, olive oil and lemon juice.

Preparation time **10 minutes + 15 minutes marinating**
Total cooking time **10 minutes**
Makes 16

2 fillets red mullet or goatfish, about 170 g (5¹/2 oz), skinned and deboned
I clove garlic
2 tablespoons olive oil
4 slices sandwich bread, crusts removed
75 g (2¹/4 oz) tapenade
16 pink peppercorns
16 sprigs of fresh dill
small wedges of lemon, to garnish

1 Preheat the oven to hot 220°C (425°F/Gas 7). Cut each fish fillet into eight pieces. Place the garlic clove in the olive oil, toss into the fish and leave to marinate for 15 minutes.
2 Toast the bread and spread with a thin layer of tapenade. Cut each slice diagonally into four triangles and arrange on a baking tray. Place the marinated fish on the prepared toasts and, just before serving, place in the oven for 2–3 minutes, or until the fish is just cooked (it will flake when lightly pressed with a fork).
3 Remove from the oven and transfer to a serving tray. Place a small dot of the tapenade on the top, then a pink peppercorn in the centre. Decorate with a sprig of dill and a lemon wedge.

Parma ham and melon fingers (top) and Red mullet and tapenade on toast

Spring rolls with pork stuffing

These rolls are deep-fried, however, if you do not have a deep-fat fryer, it is possible to use a heavy-based pan. The results will be just as good, but extreme care should be taken with the hot oil.

Preparation time **40 minutes + 30 minutes chilling**
Total cooking time **40 minutes**
Makes about **40**

2 tablespoons oil
250 g (8 oz) minced pork
1/2 Chinese cabbage, shredded finely (see page 63)
2 spring onions, sliced
1 teaspoon grated fresh ginger
30 g (1 oz) bamboo shoots, finely chopped
3 button mushrooms, thinly sliced
1/2 teaspoon dried sage
1 teaspoon soy sauce
2 teaspoons cornflour
20 spring roll wrappers, about 20 cm (8 inches) square
soy sauce, to serve

1 Heat the oil in a large pan over high heat, add the pork and cook for about 3 minutes, stirring continuously. Transfer the meat to a bowl to cool. When cool, add the Chinese cabbage, spring onion, ginger, bamboo shoots, mushrooms, dried sage, soy sauce and 1 teaspoon of the cornflour. Stir to combine well, then season to taste with salt and pepper.

2 Add a little water to the remaining teaspoon of cornflour to make a paste and set aside. Prepare the spring rolls by following the method in the Chef's techniques on page 63. Place in the refrigerator to chill for at least 30 minutes before cooking.

3 Heat the oil in a deep-fat fryer or deep saucepan (see Chef's techniques, page 63). Fry the spring rolls in batches of four or five for about 3–5 minutes, or until cooked and golden brown. The spring rolls will float to the surface of the oil when cooked. Remove and drain on crumpled paper towels. Serve the spring rolls hot with the soy sauce.

Chef's tip These could also be made using filo pastry. Brush sheets of filo with melted butter, wrap around the filling, then bake in a moderately hot 200°C (400°F/ Gas 6) oven for 10 minutes, or until golden and crisp.

Chef's techniques

♦

Preparing pancakes

These pancakes can be rolled up with any moist filling, such as herby cream cheese and smoked fish.

Using a fork or chopsticks, slowly incorporate the flour into the water until a soft dough forms. Turn out onto a floured surface and knead for 5 minutes, or until smooth. Cover and set aside for 15 minutes.

Divide the dough into six and roll into balls. Flatten one ball, brush lightly with some sesame oil and place another flattened round of dough on top. Roll out into 21 cm (8^1/2 inch) circles, about 1 mm (^{1}/16 inch) thick.

Heat a dry frying pan over medium-high heat. Place a pancake in the hot pan and cook for 50–60 seconds, or until blistered and coloured. Flip over and cook for another 30–40 seconds.

Transfer the pancake to a plate and while it is still hot, carefully peel it apart, being careful of any hot steam. Repeat with the remaining pancakes.

Grilling capsicums

Grilling capsicums allows you to remove their skins and produces a delicious sweet flavour.

Preheat a grill. Cut the capsicums in half and remove the seeds and membrane.

Grill the capsicums until the skin blisters and blackens. Place in a plastic bag and allow to cool. When cool, peel off the skin.

Threading satay beef

This is an attractive way to present satays, although the meat can also be cut into small cubes.

If using wooden skewers, soak in cold water for about 1 hour before using to prevent them from burning. Cut the beef into 5 mm (^{1}/4 inch) strips. Thread onto wooden skewers.

Choux pastry

Little balls of light choux pastry can be filled or sandwiched together with savoury or sweet fillings.

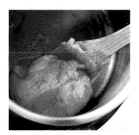

Once the butter has melted, bring to the boil, then add all the flour and stir continuously with a wooden spoon until the mixture rolls off the side of the pan. Remove from the heat and cool until just warm.

Transfer the mixture to a medium bowl. Add the egg in six additions, beating well between each addition until the mixture thickens.

Rolling up spring rolls

Spring roll wrappers are very delicate and should be covered with a damp cloth while you work.

Shred the cabbage leaves by rolling them up tightly and cutting finely.

Cut each spring roll wrapper in half. Divide the filling between each spring roll wrapper and roll up tightly. Seal the edges using cornflour paste.

Layering filo pastry

Purchased filo is very easy to use as long as you keep it covered to prevent it from drying out.

Place the sheets of filo pastry on a work surface and cover with a damp tea towel. Work with one sheet at a time, keeping the rest covered to stop them from drying out.

Brush the first sheet with melted butter, then place another sheet on top and brush again with melted butter. Repeat until you have the number of layers specified in the recipe.

Deep-frying

Fill the fryer only one-third full of oil: do not leave it unattended. Dry food thoroughly before deep-frying

Preheat the oil in a deep-fat fryer or deep saucepan to 180°C (350°F). Place a bread cube in the oil: if it sizzles and turns golden brown in 15 seconds, the oil is hot enough.

Published in 1998 by Merehurst Limited, Ferry House, 51–57 Lacy Road, Putney, London SW15 1PR.

Merehurst Limited, Murdoch Books and Le Cordon Bleu thank the 32 masterchefs of all the Le Cordon Bleu Schools, whose knowledge and expertise have made this book possible, especially: Chef Cliche (MOF), Chef Terrien, Chef Boucheret, Chef Duchêne (MOF), Chef Guillut, Chef Steneck, Paris; Chef Males, Chef Walsh, Chef Hardy, London; Chef Chantefort, Chef Bertin, Chef Jambert, Chef Honda, Tokyo; Chef Salembien, Chef Boutin, Chef Harris, Sydney; Chef Lawes, Adelaide; Chef Guiet, Chef Denis, Ottawa. Of the many students who helped the Chefs test each recipe, a special mention to graduates David Welch and Allen Wertheim. A very special acknowledgment to Directors Susan Eckstein, Great Britain, and Kathy Shaw, Paris, who have been responsible for the coordination of the Le Cordon Bleu team throughout this series.

Managing Editor: Kay Halsey
Series Concept, Design and Art Direction: Juliet Cohen
Food Director: Jody Vassallo
Food Editors: Kathy Knudsen, Tracy Rutherford
Designer: Annette Fitzgerald
Photographer: Andre Martin
Food Stylist: Jane Hann
Food Preparation: Alison Turner
Chef's Techniques Photographer: Reg Morrison
Home Economists: Kathy Knudsen, Justine Poole, Zoe Radze, Alison Turner

Creative Director: Marylouise Brammer
International Sales Director: Mark Newman
CEO & Publisher: Anne Wilson

ISBN 1 85391 750 8

Printed by Toppan Printing (S) Pte Ltd
First Printed 1998
©Design and photography Murdoch Books® 1998
©Text Le Cordon Bleu 1998

A catalogue record for this book is available from the British Library.

Distributed in the UK by D Services, 6 Euston Street, Freemen's Common, Leicester LE2 7SS Tel 0116-254-7671
Fax 0116-254-4670.
Distributed in Canada by Whitecap (Vancouver) Ltd, 351 Lynn Avenue, North Vancouver, BC V7J 2C4
Tel 604-980-9852 Fax 604-980-8197 or Whitecap (Ontario) Ltd, 47 Coldwater Road, North York, ON M3B 1Y8
Tel 416-444-3442 Fax 416-444-6630
Published and distributed in Australia by Murdoch Books®, 45 Jones Street, Ultimo NSW 2007

The Publisher and Le Cordon Bleu wish to thank Carole Sweetnam for her help with this series.
Front cover: Mini blinis with caviar

IMPORTANT INFORMATION

CONVERSION GUIDE

1 cup = 250 ml (8 fl oz)
1 Australian tablespoon = 20 ml (4 teaspoons)
1 UK tablespoon = 15 ml (3 teaspoons)

NOTE: We have used 20 ml tablespoons. If you are using a 15 ml tablespoon, for most recipes the difference will be negligible. For recipes using baking powder, gelatine, bicarbonate of soda and flour, add an extra teaspoon for each tablespoon specified.

CUP CONVERSIONS—DRY INGREDIENTS

1 cup flour, plain or self-raising = 125 g (4 oz)
1 cup sugar, caster = 250 g (8 oz)
1 cup breadcrumbs, dry = 125 g (4 oz)

IMPORTANT: Those who might be at risk from the effects of salmonella food poisoning (the elderly, pregnant women, young children and those suffering from immune deficiency diseases) should consult their GP with any concerns about eating raw eggs.